# The Meaning of Percent

Allan D. Suter

 McGraw Hill **Contemporary**

*Series Editor:* Mitch Rosin
*Executive Editor:* Linda Kwil
*Production Manager:* Genevieve Kelley
*Marketing Manager:* Sean Klunder
*Cover Design:* Steve Strauss, ¡Think! Design

 **Contemporary**

Send all inquiries to:
McGraw-Hill/Contemporary
130 East Randolph Street, Suite 400
Chicago, Illinois 60601

ISBN: 0-07-287112-1

Printed in the United States of America.

1 2 3 4 5 6 7 8 9 10  QPD/QPD  09 08 07 06 05 04 03

*The McGraw·Hill Companies*

1. 90% means _____ out of 100.

   Answer: _____

2. 75 out of 100 is the same as _____%.

   Answer: _____

3. One whole is the same as _____%.

   Answer: _____

4. Write $\frac{3}{4}$ as a percent.

   Answer: _____

5. Write 30% as a fraction and simplify.

   Answer: _____

6. Change 44% to a fraction and simplify.

   Answer: _____

7. Write $\frac{7}{20}$ as a percent.

   Answer: _____

8. Change $\frac{3}{8}$ to a percent.

   Answer: _____

9. Write 240% as a mixed number and simplify.

   Answer: _____

10. Write $3\frac{1}{4}$ as a percent.

    Answer: _____

**11.** Write the whole number 5 as a percent.

Answer: _____

**12.** Write .05 as a percent.

Answer: _____

**13.** Change 25% to a decimal.

Answer: _____

**14.** What is .8 as a percent?

Answer: _____

**15.** Write 68% as a decimal.

Answer: _____

**16.** Write 2.75 as a percent.

Answer: _____

**17.** If $\frac{1}{4}$ of Carolyn's budget goes for rent, what percent of her budget goes for rent?

Answer: _____

**18.** Alfonso got 3 out of 10 questions wrong on an English quiz. What percent of the questions did he get right?

Answer: _____

**19.** Martina saves $1 out of every $10 that she makes. What percent does she save?

Answer: _____

**20.** If 3 out of every 4 homes in Middleville have Internet access, what percent of the homes have Internet access?

Answer: _____

# Evaluation Chart

On the following chart, circle the number of any problem you missed. The column after the problem number tells you the pages where those problems are taught. Based on your score, your teacher may ask you to study specific sections of this book. However, to thoroughly review your skills, begin with Unit 1 on page 7.

| Skill Area | Pretest Problem Number | Skill Section | Review Page |
|---|---|---|---|
| Meaning of Percent | 1, 2, 3 | 7–17 | 18 |
| Fractions and Percent | 4, 5, 6, 7, 8 | 19–34<br>61–65 | 35<br>66 |
| Percents Greater Than 100 | 9, 10, 11 | 36–40 | 41 |
| Percents and Decimals | 13, 15, 16 | 42–50 | 51 |
| Decimals, Fractions and Percents | 12, 14 | 52–58 | 59 |
| Percent Problem Solving | 17, 18, 19, 20 | 67–73 | 74 |

# What Is Percent?

Knowing how to work with percents is a very useful skill. Percents are used in sales, taxes, sports, and in many other ways.

> **Percent** is a special ratio comparing a number to 100.

1. In the picture _____ out of 100 squares are shaded.

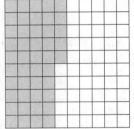

2. What ratio is shown in the picture? $\dfrac{\boxed{\phantom{0}}}{100}$

3. Express your answer to question 2 as a percent. ___45___ %

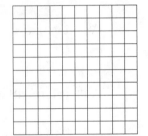

4. Shade 15 out of the 100 squares.

5. What ratio is shown in the picture? $\dfrac{\boxed{\phantom{0}}}{100}$

6. Write the ratio as a percent. _____ %
   fill in

---

> *Percent* means *parts out of 100* or *per hundred*.

50% means ___50___ out of every 100.

7. 25% means _____ out of every 100.

8. 15% means _____ out of every 100.

9. 75% means _____ out of every 100.

10. 90% means _____ out of every 100.

11. 5% means _____ out of every 100.

12. 1% means _____ out of every 100.

# Shade the Percents

1. Shade 30 out of the 100 squares.

2. What ratio is shown in the picture? /100

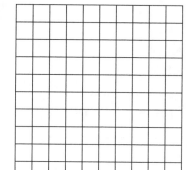

3. Write the ratio as a percent. _____%

4. What percent is not shaded? _____%

5. What percent shows the total of the shaded and the unshaded squares? _____%

---

6. Shade 65 out of the 100 squares.

7. What ratio is shown in the picture?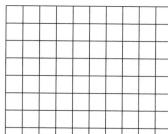

8. Write the ratio as a percent. _____%

9. What percent is not shaded? _____%

10. What percent shows the total of the shaded and the unshaded parts? _____%

---

11. Shade 87 out of the 100 squares.

12. What ratio is shown in the picture?

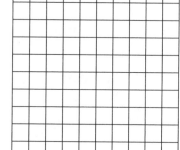

13. Write the ratio as a percent. _____%

14. What percent is not shaded? _____%

15. What percent shows the total of the shaded and the unshaded parts? _____%

# Understanding Percent

Remember: *Percent* means *parts out of 100.*

Example: 30% means __30__ out of 100 or $\frac{30}{100}$

1. 45% means __45__ out of 100 or $\frac{\square}{100}$    3. 55% means ___ out of 100 or $\frac{\square}{100}$

2. 60% means ___ out of 100 or $\frac{\square}{\square}$    4. 5% means ___ out of 100 or $\frac{\square}{\square}$

---

5. 95 out of 100 = $\frac{\square}{\square}$ = ___%    7. 50 out of 100 = $\frac{\square}{\square}$ = ___%

6. 100 out of 100 = $\frac{\square}{\square}$ = ___%    8. 75 out of 100 = $\frac{\square}{\square}$ = ___%

---

9. $\frac{33}{100}$ means ___ out of ___
   or ___%

10. $\frac{20}{100}$ means ___ out of ___
    or ___%

11. $\frac{10}{100}$ means ___ out of ___
    or ___%

12. $\frac{18}{100}$ means ___ out of ___
    or ___%

# Percent Means Parts Out of 100

How many parts are shaded out of 100?

**1.**

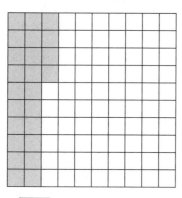

$\dfrac{\boxed{\phantom{00}}}{100}$ = _____ %

**2.**

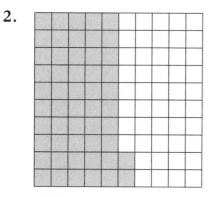

$\dfrac{\boxed{\phantom{00}}}{100}$ = _____ %

**3.**

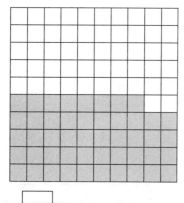

$\dfrac{\boxed{\phantom{00}}}{100}$ = _____ %

**4.**

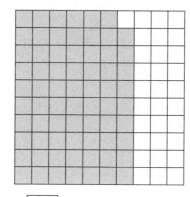

$\dfrac{\boxed{\phantom{00}}}{100}$ = _____ %

**5.**

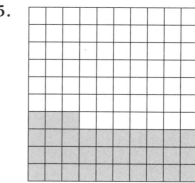

$\dfrac{\boxed{\phantom{00}}}{100}$ = _____ %

**6.**

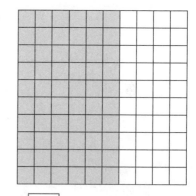

$\dfrac{\boxed{\phantom{00}}}{100}$ = _____ %

# Shade the Squares

### Shade 15 squares.

**1.**

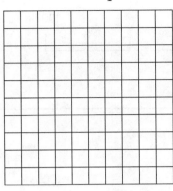

$$\frac{\boxed{\phantom{0}}}{100} = \underline{\hspace{1.5cm}}\%$$

### Shade 75 squares.

**2.**

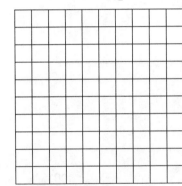

$$\frac{\boxed{\phantom{0}}}{100} = \underline{\hspace{1.5cm}}\%$$

### Shade 37 squares.

**3.**

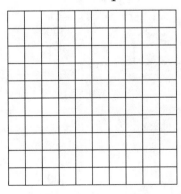

$$\frac{\boxed{\phantom{0}}}{100} = \underline{\hspace{1.5cm}}\%$$

### Shade 85 squares.

**4.**

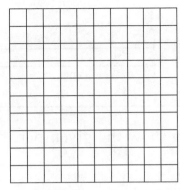

$$\frac{\boxed{\phantom{0}}}{100} = \underline{\hspace{1.5cm}}\%$$

### Shade 28 squares.

**5.**

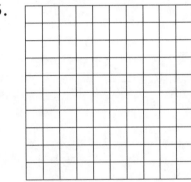

$$\frac{\boxed{\phantom{0}}}{100} = \underline{\hspace{1.5cm}}\%$$

### Shade 55 squares.

**6.**

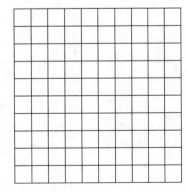

$$\frac{\boxed{\phantom{0}}}{100} = \underline{\hspace{1.5cm}}\%$$

# Number Lines

Show the given percent on the number line.

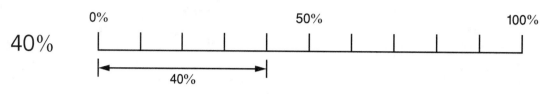

40%

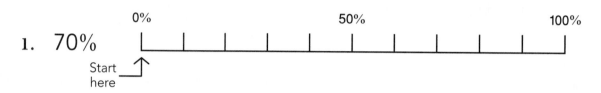

40%

---

Draw a line to show the given percent. Start at 0%.

**1.** 70%

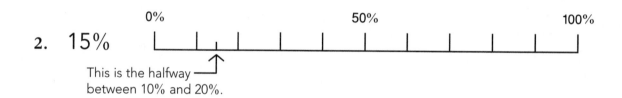

Start here

**2.** 15%

This is the halfway between 10% and 20%.

**3.** 95%

**4.** 35%

**5.** 20%

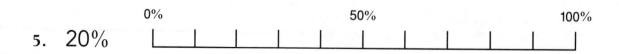

# One Hundred Percent Equals One

A. Shade all 100 sections in the large square.

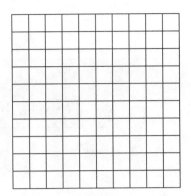

B. What percent of the square is shaded? _____%

C. $1 = \frac{100}{100} = $ _____%

         ↑——— the whole square

---

What percent is **not** shaded?

1.
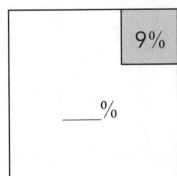
50%   _____% 
fill in

2.
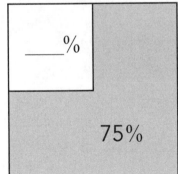
_____%
75%

3.
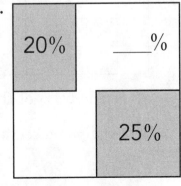
9%
_____%

4.
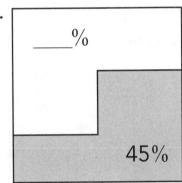
_____%
45%

5.
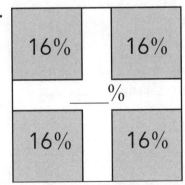
16%   16%
_____%
16%   16%

6.
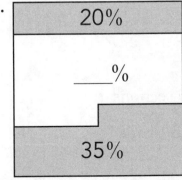
20%
_____%
35%

7.
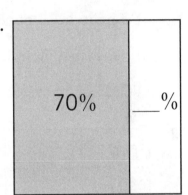
70%   _____%

8.
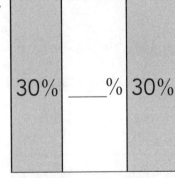
30%   _____%   30%

9.
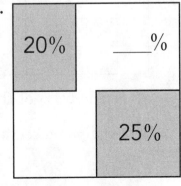
20%   _____%
25%

# Fifty Percent

A. $\dfrac{1}{2} = \dfrac{}{100} = \underline{\hspace{1cm}}$ % _fill in_

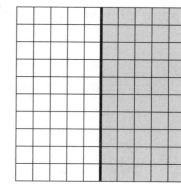

$\dfrac{1}{2}$          $\dfrac{1}{2}$

> $\dfrac{1}{2}$ or 50% of anything is the same as dividing it by 2.

---

1.

   a) Shade 50% of the 6 circles.

   b) How many circles are shaded? _____

   c) 50% of 6 = _____

2.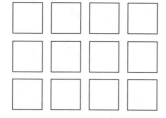

   a) Shade 50% of the 12 squares.

   b) How many squares are shaded? _____

   c) 50% of 12 = _____

3.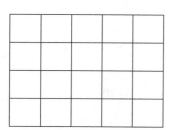

   a) Shade 50% of the 20 sections.

   b) How many sections are shaded? _____

   c) 50% of 20 = _____

4. 50% of 10 = _____

5. 50% of 16 = _____

6. 50% of 30 = _____

7. 50% of 24 = _____

8. 50% of 18 = _____

9. 50% of 50 = _____

10. 50% of 40 = _____

# Twenty-Five Percent

**A.** $\dfrac{1}{4} = \dfrac{\boxed{\phantom{0}}}{100} = \underline{\hspace{2cm}}\%$

$\underset{\text{fill in}}{}$

$\dfrac{1}{4}$ or 25% of anything is the same as dividing it by 4.

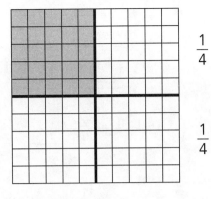

---

**1.**

**a)** Shade 25% of the 8 squares.

**b)** How many squares are shaded? _____

**c)** 25% of 8 = _____

**2.**

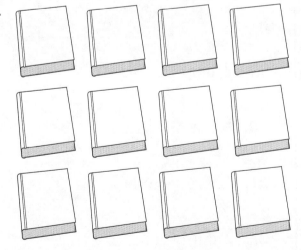

**a)** Circle 25% of the books.

**b)** How many books are circled? _____

**c)** 25% of 12 = _____

**3.** 25% of 32 = _____

**4.** 25% of 16 = _____

**5.** 25% of 20 = _____

**6.** 25% of 40 = _____

**7.** 25% of 24 = _____

**8.** 25% of 36 = _____

**9.** 25% of 4 = _____

**10.** 25% of 28 = _____

# What Does the Percent Mean?

50% means:

$$\boxed{50 \text{ out of } 100}$$

1. 1 out of ___2___
   $\frac{1}{2} = \frac{50}{100}$

2. 5 out of _____
   $\frac{1}{2} = \frac{5}{?}$

3. _____ out of 20
   $\frac{1}{2} = \frac{?}{20}$

4. 15 out of _____

5. _____ out of 18

6. _____ out of 50

10% means:

$$\boxed{10 \text{ out of } 100}$$

13. ___1___ out of 10

14. 3 out of _____
    $\frac{1}{10} = \frac{3}{?}$

15. _____ out of 20

16. _____ out of 80

17. 5 out of _____

18. _____ out of 90

25% means:

$$\boxed{25 \text{ out of } 100}$$

7. ___1___ out of 4
   $\frac{1}{4} = \frac{25}{100}$

8. _____ out of 8
   $\frac{1}{4} = \frac{?}{8}$

9. 5 out of _____

10. 10 out of _____

11. _____ out of 12

12. 4 out of _____

20% means:

$$\boxed{20 \text{ out of } 100}$$

19. 1 out of ___5___

20. 5 out of _____
    $\frac{1}{5} = \frac{5}{?}$

21. _____ out of 10

22. 7 out of _____

23. _____ out of 15

24. 9 out of _____

# More Percent Meanings

60% means:

60 out of 100

1. 3 out of ___5___

2. 6 out of _____

3. _____ out of 20

4. 24 out of _____

5. _____ out of 50

6. 36 out of _____

80% means:

80 out of 100

13. 4 out of _____

14. _____ out of 10

15. 12 out of _____

16. _____ out of 25

17. 36 out of _____

18. _____ out of 35

40% means:

40 out of 100

7. _____ out of 5

8. _____ out of 50

9. 4 out of _____

10. 16 out of _____

11. 8 out of _____

12. _____ out of 30

75% means:

75 out of 100

19. 3 out of _____

20. _____ out of 8

21. 15 out of _____

22. _____ out of 28

23. _____ out of 12

24. 18 out of _____

# Meaning of Percent Review

Solve each problem.

1. 35% means _____ out of every 100.

2. 25% means _____ out of every 100.

---

What percent is not shaded?

3.

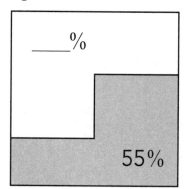

____%

55%

4.

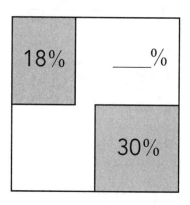

18%    ____%

30%

5.

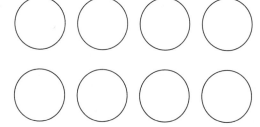

Shade 25% of the circles.

25% of 8 is _____.

---

6. What is 50% of 26?

Answer: _____

7. What is 50% of 74?

Answer: _____

8. What is 25% of 36?

Answer: _____

9. What is 25% of 44?

Answer: _____

10. What is 60% of 5?

Answer: _____

# Common Fractions and Percents

| Commonly Used Fractions and Percent Equivalents | |
|---|---|
| $\frac{1}{2} = 50\%$ | $\frac{1}{3} = 33\frac{1}{3}\%$ |
| $\frac{1}{4} = 25\%$ | $\frac{2}{3} = 66\frac{2}{3}\%$ |
| $\frac{3}{4} = 75\%$ | $\frac{1}{10} = 10\%$ |

Use the chart above to find the percent shaded in each figure.

1.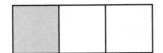

$$\frac{33\frac{1}{3}}{}\%$$
Think: $\frac{1}{3} = 33\frac{1}{3}\%$

4.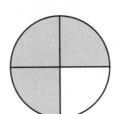

_____ %

7.

_____ %

2.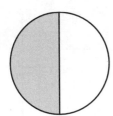

_____ %

5.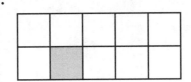

_____ %

8.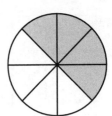

_____ %

3.

_____ %

6.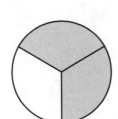

_____ %

9.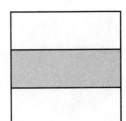

_____ %

# Rename as a Percent

For each figure:

  **1.** Using a fraction, name the fractional part that is shaded.

  **2.** Rename the fraction in hundredths.

  **3.** Write as a percent.

**1.**

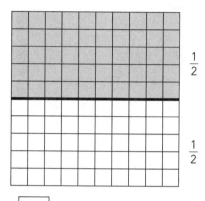

$$\frac{\boxed{\phantom{0}}}{2} = \frac{50}{100} = \underline{\hspace{1cm}}\%$$

**3.**

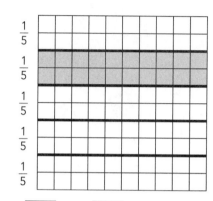

$$\frac{\boxed{\phantom{0}}}{5} = \frac{\boxed{\phantom{0}}}{100} = \underline{\hspace{1cm}}\%$$

**2.**

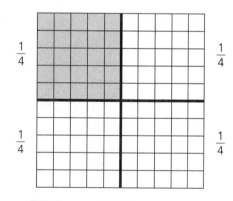

$$\frac{\boxed{\phantom{0}}}{4} = \frac{\boxed{\phantom{0}}}{100} = \underline{\hspace{1cm}}\%$$

**4.**

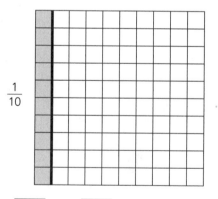

$$\frac{\boxed{\phantom{0}}}{10} = \frac{\boxed{\phantom{0}}}{100} = \underline{\hspace{1cm}}\%$$

# Ratios to Percents

Remember: A **ratio** is a comparison of two numbers.

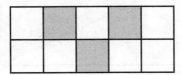

1. _____ out of 10 sections (squares) are shaded.

2. The ratio is $\dfrac{\boxed{\phantom{0}}}{10}$ .

3. At the same rate, how many sections out of 100 would be shaded? _____

   Think: $\dfrac{3}{10} \begin{matrix} \times \\ \times \end{matrix} \boxed{\dfrac{10}{10}} = \dfrac{\boxed{\phantom{0}}}{100}$ , which equals _____ %

4. _____ out of 10 sections are not shaded.

5. What percent is not shaded? _____ %

---

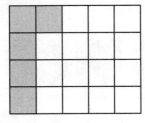

6. _____ out of 20 sections are shaded.

7. The ratio is $\dfrac{\boxed{\phantom{0}}}{20}$ .

8. At the same rate, how many sections out of 100 would be shaded? _____

   Think: $\dfrac{5}{20} \begin{matrix} \times \\ \times \end{matrix} \boxed{\dfrac{5}{5}} = \dfrac{\boxed{\phantom{0}}}{100}$ , which equals _____ %

9. _____ out of 20 sections are not shaded.

10. What percent is not shaded? _____ %

# Apply Your Skills

What percent of each figure is shaded?

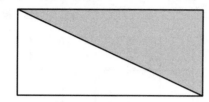

**1.** Shaded parts ⟶ $\dfrac{1}{2} \times \dfrac{\boxed{50}}{\boxed{50}} = \dfrac{\square}{100} = $ _____ %

Total parts ⟶

**2.** Shaded parts ⟶ $\dfrac{\square}{4} \times \dfrac{\boxed{1}}{\boxed{25}} = \dfrac{\square}{100} = $ _____ %

Total parts ⟶

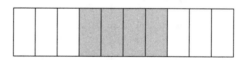

**3.** Shaded parts ⟶ $\dfrac{\square}{\square} \times \dfrac{\boxed{1}}{\boxed{10}} = \dfrac{\square}{100} = $ _____ %

Total parts ⟶

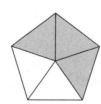

**4.** Shaded parts ⟶ $\dfrac{\square}{\square} \times \dfrac{\boxed{1}}{\boxed{20}} = \dfrac{\square}{100} = $ _____ %

Total parts ⟶

# Use the Pictures

For each figure, write a fraction to show the number of shaded parts to total parts. Change the fraction to a percent.

1.  Shaded parts → $\dfrac{\boxed{\phantom{0}}}{\boxed{\phantom{0}}}$ = $\dfrac{\boxed{\phantom{0}}}{100}$ = _____ %
    Total parts →

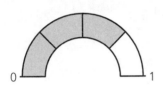

2.  Shaded parts → $\dfrac{\boxed{\phantom{0}}}{\boxed{\phantom{0}}}$ = $\dfrac{\boxed{\phantom{0}}}{100}$ = _____ %
    Total parts →

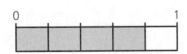

3.  Shaded parts → $\dfrac{\boxed{\phantom{0}}}{\boxed{\phantom{0}}}$ = $\dfrac{\boxed{\phantom{0}}}{\boxed{\phantom{0}}}$ = _____ %
    Total parts →

4.  Shaded parts → $\dfrac{\boxed{\phantom{0}}}{\boxed{\phantom{0}}}$ = $\dfrac{\boxed{\phantom{0}}}{\boxed{\phantom{0}}}$ = _____ %
    Total parts →

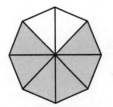

5.  $\dfrac{6}{8}$ = $\dfrac{3}{4}$ = $\dfrac{\boxed{\phantom{0}}}{100}$ = _____ %
    simplify

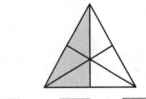

6.  $\dfrac{\boxed{\phantom{0}}}{\boxed{\phantom{0}}}$ = $\dfrac{\boxed{\phantom{0}}}{\boxed{\phantom{0}}}$ = $\dfrac{\boxed{\phantom{0}}}{100}$ = _____ %
    simplify

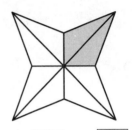

7.  $\dfrac{\boxed{\phantom{0}}}{\boxed{\phantom{0}}}$ = $\dfrac{\boxed{\phantom{0}}}{\boxed{\phantom{0}}}$ = $\dfrac{\boxed{\phantom{0}}}{100}$ = _____ %
    simplify

8.  $\dfrac{\boxed{\phantom{0}}}{\boxed{\phantom{0}}}$ = $\dfrac{\boxed{\phantom{0}}}{\boxed{\phantom{0}}}$ = $\dfrac{\boxed{\phantom{0}}}{100}$ = _____ %
    simplify

# Shade the Percents

Count the number of parts in each figure. Use your knowledge of fractions to shade in the percent asked for in the problem.

**1.**

$\frac{1}{2}$ or 50%

(Think: $\frac{1}{2}$ of 6 = 3)

**3.**

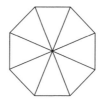

$\frac{3}{8}$ or $37\frac{1}{2}$%

**2.**

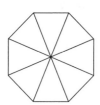

$\frac{1}{4}$ or 25%

**4.**

$\frac{3}{5}$ or 60%

---

For each figure, draw lines from each corner to the center. Shade in the percent asked for in the problem.

**5.**

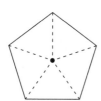

$\frac{2}{5}$ or 40%

**7.**

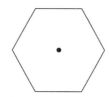

$\frac{2}{3}$ or $66\frac{2}{3}$%

**6.**

$\frac{1}{3}$ or $33\frac{1}{3}$%

**8.**

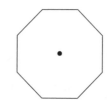

$\frac{7}{8}$ or $87\frac{1}{2}$%

# Name the Percent

For each problem, name the fractional part that is shaded or circled. Rename this part as a percent.

**1.**

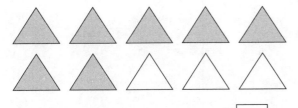

$$\text{Parts shaded} \longrightarrow \frac{7}{10} = \frac{\boxed{\phantom{0}}}{100} = \underline{\phantom{000}}\%$$
$$\text{Total parts} \longrightarrow$$

---

**2.**

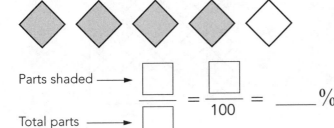

$$\text{Parts circled} \longrightarrow \frac{\boxed{\phantom{0}}}{\boxed{\phantom{0}}} = \frac{\boxed{\phantom{0}}}{100} = \underline{\phantom{000}}\%$$
$$\text{Total parts} \longrightarrow$$

---

**3.**

$$\text{Parts shaded} \longrightarrow \frac{\boxed{\phantom{0}}}{\boxed{\phantom{0}}} = \frac{\boxed{\phantom{0}}}{100} = \underline{\phantom{000}}\%$$
$$\text{Total parts} \longrightarrow$$

---

**4.**

$$\text{Parts circled} \longrightarrow \frac{\boxed{\phantom{0}}}{\boxed{\phantom{0}}} = \frac{\boxed{\phantom{0}}}{100} = \underline{\phantom{000}}\%$$
$$\text{Total parts} \longrightarrow$$

# Think It Through

1. Draw 12 small circles inside the square. Shade in 25% of them.

2. Draw a picture inside the rectangle showing the statement "80% of the 10 Xs are circled."

---

How much of each drawing is circled?

3. $\dfrac{\boxed{\phantom{0}}}{20} = \dfrac{\boxed{\phantom{0}}}{100} = \underline{\phantom{00}}\%$

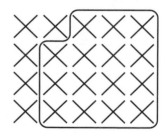

4. $\dfrac{\boxed{\phantom{0}}}{5} = \dfrac{\boxed{\phantom{0}}}{100} = \underline{\phantom{00}}\%$

5. $\dfrac{\boxed{\phantom{0}}}{\boxed{\phantom{0}}} = \dfrac{\boxed{\phantom{0}}}{\boxed{\phantom{0}}} = \dfrac{\boxed{\phantom{0}}}{100} = \underline{\phantom{00}}\%$

simplify

# Change Fractions to Percents

To change fractions to percents, first find equal fractions with denominators of 100.

**A.**  $\dfrac{1}{2} = \dfrac{50}{100} = \underset{\text{fill in}}{\underline{\hspace{1cm}}}\%$

**B.**  $\dfrac{2}{5} = \underset{\text{fill in}}{\underline{\hspace{1cm}}}\%$      $\dfrac{2}{5} \times \dfrac{20}{20} = \dfrac{40}{100} = 40\%$

Think: $100 \div 5 = 20$

**C.**  $\dfrac{3}{4} = \underset{\text{fill in}}{\underline{\hspace{1cm}}}\%$      $\dfrac{3}{4} \times \dfrac{\square}{25} = \dfrac{\square}{100} = \underline{\hspace{1cm}}\%$

Think: $100 \div 4 = 25$

---

Change the fractions to percents.

**1.** $\dfrac{2}{10} = \dfrac{\square}{100} = \underline{\hspace{1cm}}\%$

Think: $100 \div 10 = 10$

**2.** $\dfrac{3}{5} = \dfrac{\square}{100} = \underline{\hspace{1cm}}\%$

**3.** $\dfrac{1}{4} = \dfrac{\square}{100} = \underline{\hspace{1cm}}\%$

**4.** $\dfrac{7}{10} = \dfrac{\square}{100} = \underline{\hspace{1cm}}\%$

**5.** $\dfrac{1}{25} = \dfrac{\square}{100} = \underline{\hspace{1cm}}\%$

**6.** $\dfrac{4}{5} = \dfrac{\square}{100} = \underline{\hspace{1cm}}\%$

**7.** $\dfrac{1}{20} = \dfrac{\square}{100} = \underline{\hspace{1cm}}\%$

**8.** $\dfrac{5}{5} = \dfrac{\square}{100} = \underline{\hspace{1cm}}\%$

**9.** $\dfrac{7}{20} = \dfrac{\square}{100} = \underline{\hspace{1cm}}\%$

**10.** $\dfrac{9}{50} = \dfrac{\square}{100} = \underline{\hspace{1cm}}\%$

# Percent Wise

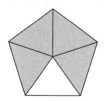

1. What percent of the figure is shaded? _____%

2. What percent is not shaded? _____%

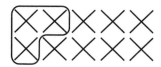

3. What percent of the Xs are circled? _____%

4. What percent of the Xs are not circled? _____%

5. What percent of the Xs are circled? _____%

6. What percent of the Xs are not circled? _____%

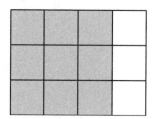

7. What percent of the figure is shaded? _____%

8. What percent is not shaded? _____%

# Show What Percent Is Shaded

1.

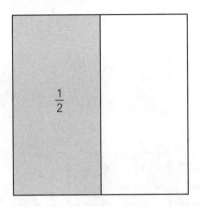

a) What percent is shaded? <u>50%</u>

b) What percent is not shaded? _____

2.

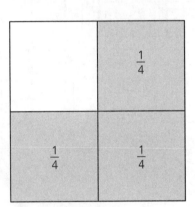

a) What percent is shaded? _____

b) What percent is not shaded? _____

3.

a) What percent is shaded? _____

b) What percent is not shaded? _____

4.

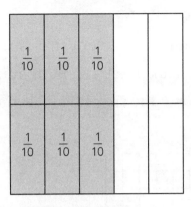

a) What percent is shaded? _____

b) What percent is not shaded? _____

5.

a) What percent is shaded? _____

b) What percent is not shaded? _____

6.

a) What percent is shaded? _____

b) What percent is not shaded? _____

# Rename Percents as Fractions

For each figure:

1. Name the percent that is shaded.
2. Rename the fraction in hundredths.
3. Write the simplified fraction.

**1.**

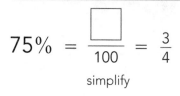

$$75\% \ = \ \frac{\boxed{\phantom{00}}}{100} \ = \ \frac{3}{4}$$

simplify

**3.**

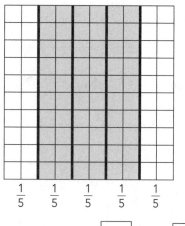

$$\rule{2cm}{0.4pt}\% \ = \ \frac{\boxed{\phantom{00}}}{100} \ = \ \frac{\boxed{\phantom{0}}}{\boxed{\phantom{0}}}$$

simplify

**2.**

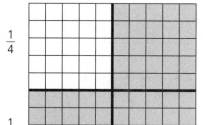

$$\rule{2cm}{0.4pt}\% \ = \ \frac{\boxed{\phantom{00}}}{100} \ = \ \frac{\boxed{\phantom{0}}}{\boxed{\phantom{0}}}$$

simplify

**4.**

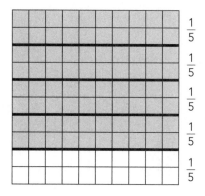

$$\rule{2cm}{0.4pt}\% \ = \ \frac{\boxed{\phantom{00}}}{100} \ = \ \frac{\boxed{\phantom{0}}}{\boxed{\phantom{0}}}$$

simplify

# Percents Are Special Ratios

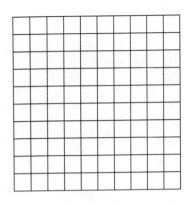

1. a) Shade in the squares to show that 60 out of 100 sections are shaded.

   b) What percent is shaded? _____ %

   c) What ratio is shown in the picture? $\frac{\boxed{\phantom{00}}}{100}$

   d) Simplify the ratio: $\frac{60}{100} = \frac{\boxed{\phantom{00}}}{\boxed{\phantom{00}}}$

---

2. Circle the simplified ratio that represents the statement below:

   "35% of the sections are shaded."

   $\frac{100}{35}$  $\frac{7}{20}$  $\frac{7}{13}$

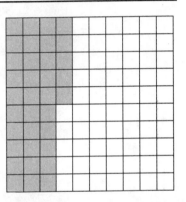

---

3. Circle the simplified ratio that represents the statement below:

   "40% of the sections are shaded."

   $\frac{2}{5}$  $\frac{10}{4}$  $\frac{5}{2}$

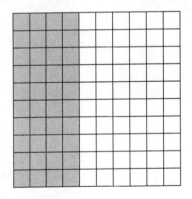

---

4. Circle the simplified ratio that represents the statement below:

   "45% of the sections are shaded."

   $\frac{20}{9}$  $\frac{9}{20}$  $\frac{12}{25}$

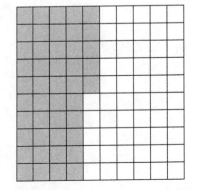

# Change Percents to Fractions

| EXAMPLE | STEP 1 | STEP 2 |
|---|---|---|
| Change 25% to a fraction. | Drop the percent sign, and write the number over 100. | Simplify the fraction. |
| | $\dfrac{25}{100}$ | $\dfrac{25}{100} \div \dfrac{25}{25} = \dfrac{1}{4}$ |

Change the percents to fractions and simplify.

1. $20\% = \dfrac{20}{100} \div \dfrac{20}{20} = \dfrac{1}{5}$
   simplify

2. $10\% = \dfrac{10}{100} \div \dfrac{10}{10} = \dfrac{\square}{\square}$

3. $30\% = \dfrac{\square}{100} = \dfrac{\square}{\square}$

4. $50\% = \dfrac{\square}{100} = \dfrac{\square}{\square}$

5. $70\% = \dfrac{\square}{100} = \dfrac{\square}{\square}$

6. $4\% = \dfrac{\square}{100} = \dfrac{\square}{\square}$

7. $90\% = \dfrac{\square}{100} = \dfrac{\square}{\square}$

8. $75\% = \dfrac{75}{100} \div \dfrac{25}{25} = \dfrac{3}{4}$

9. $5\% = \dfrac{5}{100} \div \dfrac{5}{5} = \dfrac{\square}{\square}$

10. $45\% = \dfrac{\square}{100} = \dfrac{\square}{\square}$

11. $80\% = \dfrac{\square}{100} = \dfrac{\square}{\square}$

12. $15\% = \dfrac{\square}{100} = \dfrac{\square}{\square}$

13. $60\% = \dfrac{\square}{100} = \dfrac{\square}{\square}$

14. $40\% = \dfrac{\square}{100} = \dfrac{\square}{\square}$

The Meaning of Percent

# Practice Changing Percents to Fractions

Study the examples.

Example 1: Since *percent* means *hundredths*, we can write 50% as $\frac{50}{100}$ or $\frac{1}{2}$.

Example 2: 2% can be written as $\frac{2}{100}$ or $\frac{1}{50}$.

Example 3: 30% can be written as $\frac{30}{100}$ or $\frac{3}{10}$.

Example 4: 5% can be written as $\frac{5}{100}$ or $\frac{1}{20}$.

---

Change each of the following percents to fractions.

| Percent | Fraction (simplified) | | Percent | Fraction (simplified) |
|---|---|---|---|---|
| 1. 25% $= \dfrac{25}{100} = \dfrac{\square}{4}$ | | | 10. 10% $= \dfrac{\square}{100} = \dfrac{\square}{\square}$ | |
| 2. 8% $= \dfrac{\square}{\square} = \dfrac{\square}{\square}$ | | | 11. 45% $= \dfrac{\square}{\square} = \dfrac{\square}{\square}$ | |
| 3. 15% $= \dfrac{\square}{\square} = \dfrac{\square}{\square}$ | | | 12. 1% $= \dfrac{\square}{\square} = \dfrac{\square}{\square}$ | |
| 4. 4% $= \dfrac{\square}{\square} = \dfrac{\square}{\square}$ | | | 13. 17% $= \dfrac{\square}{\square} = \dfrac{\square}{\square}$ | |
| 5. 75% $= \dfrac{\square}{\square} = \dfrac{\square}{\square}$ | | | 14. 22% $= \dfrac{\square}{\square} = \dfrac{\square}{\square}$ | |
| 6. 20% $= \dfrac{\square}{\square} = \dfrac{\square}{\square}$ | | | 15. 60% $= \dfrac{\square}{\square} = \dfrac{\square}{\square}$ | |
| 7. 90% $= \dfrac{\square}{\square} = \dfrac{\square}{\square}$ | | | 16. 36% $= \dfrac{\square}{\square} = \dfrac{\square}{\square}$ | |
| 8. 6% $= \dfrac{\square}{\square} = \dfrac{\square}{\square}$ | | | 17. 9% $= \dfrac{\square}{\square} = \dfrac{\square}{\square}$ | |
| 9. 12% $= \dfrac{\square}{\square} = \dfrac{\square}{\square}$ | | | 18. 28% $= \dfrac{\square}{\square} = \dfrac{\square}{\square}$ | |

# Common Equivalents

Some fractions and percents are used very often. If you learn these equivalents, it will make your work much easier.

| Memorize these common equivalents. It's worth the effort! | | | |
|---|---|---|---|
| $\frac{1}{4} = 25\%$ | $\frac{3}{4} = 75\%$ | $\frac{2}{3} = 66\frac{2}{3}\%$ | $\frac{1}{10} = 10\%$ |
| $\frac{1}{2} = 50\%$ | $\frac{1}{3} = 33\frac{1}{3}\%$ | $\frac{1}{5} = 20\%$ | $\frac{1}{8} = 12\frac{1}{2}\%$ |

After you have memorized the chart, fill in the blanks.

1. $25\% = $ _____

2. $20\% = $ _____

3. $50\% = $ _____

4. $10\% = $ _____

5. $66\frac{2}{3}\% = $ _____

6. $12\frac{1}{2}\% = $ _____

7. $75\% = $ _____

8. $33\frac{1}{3}\% = $ _____

9. $\frac{2}{3} = $ _____

10. $\frac{1}{8} = $ _____

11. $\frac{3}{4} = $ _____

12. $\frac{1}{5} = $ _____

13. $\frac{1}{10} = $ _____

14. $\frac{1}{4} = $ _____

15. $\frac{1}{3} = $ _____

16. $\frac{1}{2} = $ _____

# Fractions and Percents Review

**1.** What percent of this figure is shaded?

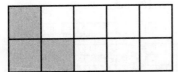

Answer: _____%

**2.** Write a fraction to represent the shaded area. Then find the percent.

$$\frac{\Box}{\Box} = \frac{\Box}{\Box} = \frac{}{100} = \_\_\_\%$$

simplify

**3.** What percent of the Xs are circled?

Answer: _____

Change the fractions to a percent.

**4.** $\frac{3}{5} = \frac{}{100} = \_\_\_\%$

**5.** $\frac{17}{25} = \frac{}{100} = \_\_\_\%$

Change each of the following percents to fractions and simplify.

**6. a)** 60%        Answer: _____

**b)** 45%        Answer: _____

**7. a)** 22%        Answer: _____

**b)** 38%        Answer: _____

**8. a)** 9%        Answer: _____

**b)** 12%        Answer: _____

Fill in the common equivalents.

**9. a)** 25% = _____

**b)** $33\frac{1}{3}\%$ = _____

**10. a)** $\frac{1}{8}$ = _____%

**b)** $\frac{1}{5}$ = _____%

# Numbers Greater Than 100%

**1.** Shade 150%

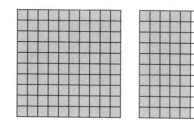

$100\% + 50\% = \underline{\quad}\%$

$1 + \dfrac{1}{2} = \dfrac{\boxed{\phantom{x}}}{\boxed{\phantom{x}}}$ 

mixed number

**4.** Shade 130%

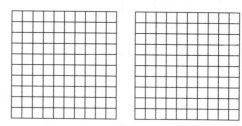

$\underline{\quad}\% + \underline{\quad}\% = \underline{\quad}\%$

$1 + \dfrac{\boxed{\phantom{x}}}{10} = \dfrac{\boxed{\phantom{x}}}{\boxed{\phantom{x}}}$

mixed number

**2.** Shade 125%

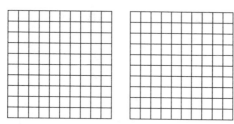

$100\% + 25\% = \underline{\quad}\%$

$1 + \dfrac{\boxed{\phantom{x}}}{4} = \dfrac{\boxed{\phantom{x}}}{\boxed{\phantom{x}}}$

**5.** Shade 120%

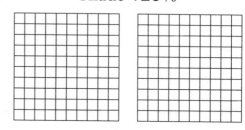

$\underline{\quad}\% + \underline{\quad}\% = \underline{\quad}\%$

$1 + \dfrac{\boxed{\phantom{x}}}{5} = \dfrac{\boxed{\phantom{x}}}{\boxed{\phantom{x}}}$

**3.** Shade 175%

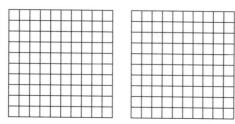

$100\% + 75\% = \underline{\quad}\%$

$1 + \dfrac{\boxed{\phantom{x}}}{4} = \dfrac{\boxed{\phantom{x}}}{\boxed{\phantom{x}}}$

**6.** Shade 190%

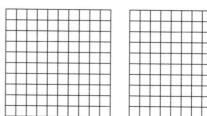

$\underline{\quad}\% + \underline{\quad}\% = \underline{\quad}\%$

$1 + \dfrac{\boxed{\phantom{x}}}{10} = \dfrac{\boxed{\phantom{x}}}{\boxed{\phantom{x}}}$

# Change Percents to Mixed Numbers

Sometimes you will need to work with more than one whole (100%). You will need to use percents greater than 100%.

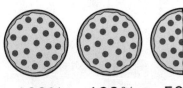     

100%  100%  50%          100%  100%  100%  100%  25%

$1 + 1 + \frac{1}{2} = 2\frac{1}{2}$       $1 + 1 + 1 + 1 + \frac{1}{4} = 4\frac{1}{4}$

---

Write the whole numbers as fractions with denominators of 100. Then write the percents.

1. $1 = \frac{100}{100} = \underline{100}\%$

2. $2 = \frac{200}{100} = \underline{200}\%$

3. $5 = \frac{\phantom{000}}{100} = \underline{\phantom{00}}\%$

4. $3 = \frac{\phantom{000}}{100} = \underline{\phantom{00}}\%$

5. $4 = \frac{\phantom{000}}{100} = \underline{\phantom{00}}\%$

6. $8 = \frac{\phantom{000}}{100} = \underline{\phantom{00}}\%$

---

Write the percents as mixed numbers.

7. $310\% = 300\% + 10\%$

$= \underline{3} + \frac{\boxed{10}}{100}$

$= \underline{3} + \frac{\boxed{1}}{\boxed{10}} = 3\frac{\boxed{1}}{\boxed{10}}$

8. $450\% = 400\% + 50\%$

$= \underline{\phantom{00}} + \frac{\boxed{\phantom{0}}}{100}$

$= \underline{\phantom{0}} + \frac{\boxed{\phantom{0}}}{\boxed{\phantom{0}}} = \underline{\phantom{0}}\frac{\boxed{\phantom{0}}}{\boxed{\phantom{0}}}$

9. $225\% = \underline{\phantom{00}}\% + \underline{\phantom{00}}\%$

$= \underline{\phantom{0}} + \frac{\boxed{\phantom{0}}}{100}$

$= \underline{\phantom{0000}}$

10. $460\% = \underline{\phantom{00}}\% + \underline{\phantom{00}}\%$

$= \underline{\phantom{0}} + \frac{\boxed{\phantom{0}}}{100}$

$= \underline{\phantom{0000}}$

11. $270\% = \underline{\phantom{00}}\% + \underline{\phantom{00}}\%$

$= \underline{\phantom{0}} + \frac{\boxed{\phantom{0}}}{100}$

$= \underline{\phantom{0000}}$

12. $580\% = \underline{\phantom{00}}\% + \underline{\phantom{00}}\%$

$= \underline{\phantom{0}} + \frac{\boxed{\phantom{0}}}{100}$

$= \underline{\phantom{0000}}$

# Practice Helps

Write the whole numbers as fractions with denominators of 100. Then write the percents.

1.  $6 = \dfrac{\phantom{00}}{100} = \underline{\phantom{00}}\%$

2.  $9 = \dfrac{\phantom{00}}{100} = \underline{\phantom{00}}\%$

3.  $7 = \dfrac{\phantom{00}}{100} = \underline{\phantom{00}}\%$

4.  $2 = \dfrac{\phantom{00}}{100} = \underline{\phantom{00}}\%$

5.  $4 = \dfrac{\phantom{00}}{100} = \underline{\phantom{00}}\%$

Write the percents as mixed numbers.

6.  $460\% = \underline{\phantom{0}}\dfrac{\square}{\square}$

7.  $380\% = \underline{\phantom{0}}\dfrac{\square}{\square}$

8.  $250\% = \underline{\phantom{0}}\dfrac{\square}{\square}$

9.  $125\% = \underline{\phantom{0}}\dfrac{\square}{\square}$

10.  $880\% = \underline{\phantom{0}}\dfrac{\square}{\square}$

# Mixed Practice

Change each percent to a fraction or mixed number and simplify answers when necessary.

1. $20\% = \dfrac{\boxed{\phantom{0}}}{100} = \dfrac{\boxed{\phantom{0}}}{\boxed{\phantom{0}}}$

   simplified

2. $275\% = 2 + \dfrac{\boxed{\phantom{0}}}{100} = \boxed{\phantom{0}}\,\dfrac{\boxed{\phantom{0}}}{4}$

3. $350\% = 3 + \dfrac{\boxed{\phantom{0}}}{100} = \boxed{\phantom{0}}\,\dfrac{\boxed{\phantom{0}}}{\boxed{\phantom{0}}}$

4. $45\% = \dfrac{\boxed{\phantom{0}}}{100} = \dfrac{\boxed{\phantom{0}}}{\boxed{\phantom{0}}}$

5. $5\% = \dfrac{\boxed{\phantom{0}}}{100} = \dfrac{\boxed{\phantom{0}}}{\boxed{\phantom{0}}}$

6. $160\% = \boxed{\phantom{0}} + \dfrac{\boxed{\phantom{0}}}{100} = \boxed{\phantom{0}}\,\dfrac{\boxed{\phantom{0}}}{5}$

7. $8\% = \dfrac{\boxed{\phantom{0}}}{100} = \dfrac{\boxed{\phantom{0}}}{25}$

8. $625\% =$

9. $10\% =$

10. $420\% =$

11. $80\% =$

12. $4\% =$

13. $105\% =$

14. $85\% =$

# More Mixed Practice

1. 15 out of 100 is what percent? _____

2. 25 out of 100 represents what percent? _____

3. What percent of the line has been marked off? _____

Complete the problems. Simplify fractions when necessary.

4. Write $\frac{1}{4}$ as a percent. _____%

5. Write 275% as a mixed number. _____

6. 2 out of 20 = _____%

7. Write 30% as a fraction. _____

8. Write $\frac{7}{10}$ as a percent. _____%

9. Write $7\frac{1}{2}$ as percent. _____%

10. Write $\frac{1}{2}$ as a percent. _____%

11. 1 out of 5 = _____%

12. Write $\frac{2}{5}$ as a percent. _____%

13. 9 out of 18 = _____%

14. Write 90% as a fraction. _____

15. 5 out of 20 = _____%

# Percent Review

1. Draw a picture inside the rectangle showing the statement: "25% of the 8 Xs are circled."

Rename each fraction as a percent.

2. $\frac{1}{2}$ = _____ %

3. $\frac{1}{4}$ = _____ %

4. $\frac{3}{4}$ = _____ %

5. $\frac{1}{5}$ = _____ %

6. $6\frac{1}{10}$ = _____ %

7. 50% of 18 = _____

8. 25% of 32 = _____
   (Think: what fraction equals 25%?)

Rename each percent as a simplified fraction or mixed number.

9. 20% = $\dfrac{\square}{\square}$ = $\dfrac{\square}{\square}$

10. 50% = $\dfrac{\square}{\square}$ = $\dfrac{\square}{\square}$

11. 250% = $\underline{\ \ }\dfrac{\square}{\square}$ = $\underline{\ \ }\dfrac{\square}{\square}$

12. 10% = $\dfrac{\square}{\square}$ = $\dfrac{\square}{\square}$

13. What percent is shaded? _____ %

14. What percent is not shaded? _____ %

15. 15 out of 30 = _____ %

16. 25 out of 25 = _____ %

17. 3 out of 30 = _____ %

18. 3 out of 12 = _____ %

# Change Percents to Decimals

Since *percent* means *parts out of 100* (hundredths), we can write 25% as $\frac{25}{100}$ or .25 (twenty-five hundredths).

Study the examples.

Example 1: 50% = 50 parts out of 100 = $\frac{50}{100}$ = .50 (fifty hundredths)

Example 2: 75% = 75 parts out of 100 = $\frac{75}{100}$ = .75 (seventy-five hundredths)

Example 3: 7% = 7 parts out of 100 = $\frac{7}{100}$ = .07 (seven hundredths)

↑ zero holds the 7 in the hundredths place

---

Write the fractions and decimal forms of the percents.

1. 10% = 10 parts out of 100 = $\frac{10}{100}$ = <u>.10</u> (ten hundredths)
   decimal

2. 85% = ☐ parts out of 100 = $\frac{\square}{100}$ = _____ (eighty-five hundredths)
   decimal

3. 33% = ☐ parts out of 100 = $\frac{\square}{100}$ = _____ (thirty-three hundredths)
   decimal

4. 40% = ☐ parts out of 100 = $\frac{\square}{100}$ = _____ (forty hundredths)
   decimal

5. 15% = ☐ parts out of 100 = $\frac{\square}{100}$ = _____ (fifteen hundredths)
   decimal

6. 5% = ☐ parts out of 100 = $\frac{\square}{100}$ = <u>.05</u> (five hundredths)
   decimal

7. 3% = ☐ parts out of 100 = $\frac{\square}{100}$ = _____ (three hundredths)
   decimal

8. 1% = ☐ part out of 100 = $\frac{\square}{100}$ = _____ (one hundredth)
   decimal

# Change to Hundredths

To change a percent to a decimal, write the percent as a fraction in hundredths, and then write it as a decimal.

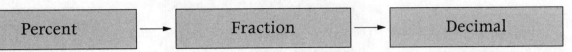

| Percent | $\rightarrow$ | Fraction | $\rightarrow$ | Decimal |

Percent means hundredths, so the second term (the denominator) is always 100.

Write the fraction as a decimal.

$$25\%$$

$$\frac{25}{100}$$

$$\frac{25}{100} = .25$$

---

Write each percent as a fraction and a decimal.

1. $15\% = \dfrac{15}{100} = \underset{\text{decimal}}{.15}$

2. $18\% = \dfrac{\square}{100} = \underset{\text{decimal}}{\underline{\hspace{1cm}}}$

3. $39\% = \dfrac{\square}{100} = \underset{\text{decimal}}{\underline{\hspace{1cm}}}$

zero holds the 7 in the hundredths place

4. $7\% = \dfrac{\square}{100} = \underset{\text{decimal}}{.0\underline{\hspace{0.6cm}}}$

5. $20\% = \dfrac{\square}{100} = \underset{\text{decimal}}{\underline{\hspace{1cm}}}$

6. $9\% = \dfrac{\square}{100} = \underset{\text{decimal}}{\underline{\hspace{1cm}}}$

7. $75\% = \dfrac{\square}{100} = \underset{\text{decimal}}{\underline{\hspace{1cm}}}$

8. $65\% = \dfrac{\square}{100} = \underset{\text{decimal}}{\underline{\hspace{1cm}}}$

9. $5\% = \dfrac{\square}{100} = \underset{\text{decimal}}{\underline{\hspace{1cm}}}$

10. $98\% = \dfrac{\square}{100} = \underset{\text{decimal}}{\underline{\hspace{1cm}}}$

11. $67\% = \dfrac{\square}{100} = \underset{\text{decimal}}{\underline{\hspace{1cm}}}$

12. $12\% = \dfrac{\square}{100} = \underset{\text{decimal}}{\underline{\hspace{1cm}}}$

13. $10\% = \dfrac{\square}{100} = \underset{\text{decimal}}{\underline{\hspace{1cm}}}$

14. $4\% = \dfrac{\square}{100} = \underset{\text{decimal}}{\underline{\hspace{1cm}}}$

# Write Percents as Decimals

Another way to change a percent to a decimal is to move the decimal point two places to the left.

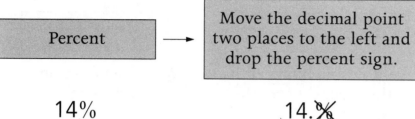

| Percent | → | Move the decimal point two places to the left and drop the percent sign. | → | Write the percent as a decimal. |

14%

14.%

.14

Decimal point starts here for a whole number.

---

Write each percent as a decimal.

1.  75% = _____
                 decimal

    75% = 75. = .___ ___
                      fill in

2.  36% = _____
                 decimal

3.  16% = _____
                 decimal

4.  44% = _____
                 decimal

5.  70% = _____
                 decimal

6.  93% = _____
                 decimal

7.  8% = _____
                decimal

8.  82% = _____
                 decimal

9.  10% = _____
                 decimal

10.  5% = _____
                decimal

11.  7% = _____
                decimal

12.  22% = _____
                  decimal

> Hint: Move the decimal 2 places to the left and add a zero to hold the tenths place.
>
> 8% = .08

# Change Percents to Mixed Decimals

To change a percent to a decimal, move the decimal point two places to the left.

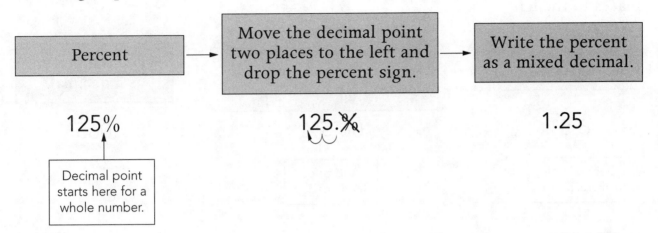

Write each percent as a mixed decimal.

1. 325% = _____ 
   <sub>decimal</sub>

   325% = 325. = ___.___ 
   <sub>fill in</sub>

2. 401% = _____ 
   <sub>decimal</sub>

3. 136% = _____ 
   <sub>decimal</sub>

4. 219% = _____ 
   <sub>decimal</sub>

5. 150% = _____ 
   <sub>decimal</sub>

6. 600% = _____ 
   <sub>decimal</sub>

7. 300% = _____ 
   <sub>decimal</sub>

8. 275% = _____ 
   <sub>decimal</sub>

9. 100% = _____ 
   <sub>decimal</sub>

10. 192% = _____ 
   <sub>decimal</sub>

11. 500% = _____ 
   <sub>decimal</sub>

12. 450% = _____ 
   <sub>decimal</sub>

# Mixed Practice

To change a percent with a decimal to a decimal, move the decimal point two places to the left.

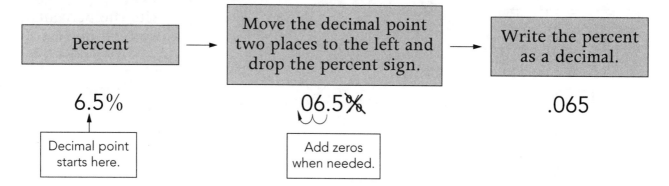

---

Change each percent to a decimal. Add zeros when needed.

1. $5.4\% =$ _____ decimal

   $5.4\% = 05.4 =$ ._ _ _ fill in

2. $21.7\% =$ _____ decimal

3. $3.68\% =$ _____ decimal

4. $45\% =$ _____ decimal

5. $300\% =$ _____ decimal

6. $9.5\% =$ _____ decimal

7. $348\% =$ _____ decimal

8. $2.6\% =$ _____ decimal

9. $350\% =$ _____ decimal

10. $1.6\% =$ _____ decimal

11. $54.3\% =$ _____ decimal

12. $19\% =$ _____ decimal

# Change Decimals to Percents

Remember: *Percent* means *parts out of 100* (hundredths).

<u>EXAMPLES</u>

.25 = 25 hundredths = 25%

.05 = 5 hundredths = 5%

---

Write each decimal as a fraction and a percent.

1.  .65 = $\dfrac{\square}{100}$ = _____ hundredths

    = _____ %

2.  .19 = $\dfrac{\square}{100}$ = _____ hundredths

    = _____ %

3.  .33 = $\dfrac{\square}{100}$ = _____ hundredths

    = _____ %

4.  .80 = $\dfrac{\square}{\square}$ = _____ hundredths

    = _____ %

5.  .01 = $\dfrac{\square}{\square}$ = _____ hundredth

    = _____ %

6.  .68 = $\dfrac{\square}{\square}$ = _____ hundredths

    = _____ %

7.  .75 = $\dfrac{\square}{\square}$ = _____ hundredths

    = _____ %

8.  .66 = $\dfrac{\square}{\square}$ = _____ hundredths

    = _____ %

9.  .08 = $\dfrac{\square}{\square}$ = _____ hundredths

    = _____ %

10. .86 = $\dfrac{\square}{\square}$ = _____ hundredths

    = _____ %

# Change One-Place Decimals to Percents

| Decimal | Change the decimal to a fraction. Rename the fraction to hundredths. | Write as a percent. |
|---|---|---|

$$.4 \qquad \frac{4}{10} \times \boxed{\frac{10}{10}} = \frac{40}{100} \qquad 40\%$$

---

Change each decimal to a percent.

1. $.8 = \frac{8}{10} \times \boxed{\frac{10}{10}} = \frac{\square}{100} = \underline{\quad}\%$

2. $.1 = \frac{\square}{10} \times \frac{10}{10} = \frac{\square}{100} = \underline{\quad}\%$

3. $.6 = \frac{\square}{10} \times \frac{\square}{\square} = \frac{\square}{100} = \underline{\quad}\%$

4. $.5 = \frac{\square}{10} \times \frac{\square}{\square} = \frac{\square}{100} = \underline{\quad}\%$

5. $.3 = \frac{\square}{10} \times \frac{\square}{\square} = \frac{\square}{100} = \underline{\quad}\%$

6. $.2 = \frac{\square}{10} \times \frac{\square}{\square} = \frac{\square}{100} = \underline{\quad}\%$

7. $.7 = \frac{\square}{10} \times \frac{\square}{\square} = \frac{\square}{100} = \underline{\quad}\%$

8. $.9 = \frac{\square}{10} \times \frac{\square}{\square} = \frac{\square}{100} = \underline{\quad}\%$

# Relating Decimals to Percents

To change a decimal to a percent, move the decimal point two places to the right and add a percent symbol.

| Decimal | → | Move the decimal point 2 places **to the right** and add a percent sign. | → | Write as a percent. |

Example 1:   .51      .51%      51%

Example 2:   3.25      3.25%      325%

Example 3:   .483      .483%      48.3%

---

Change each decimal to a percent. Remember to write a percent sign in each answer.

1.  .26 = _____%
    <sub>percent</sub>

2.  .354 = _____%
    <sub>percent</sub>

3.  1.48 = _____%
    <sub>percent</sub>

4.  .887 = _____%
    <sub>percent</sub>

5.  .36 = _____%
    <sub>percent</sub>

6.  .109 = _____%
    <sub>percent</sub>

7.  .44 = _____%
    <sub>percent</sub>

8.  .156 = _____%
    <sub>percent</sub>

9.  .78 = _____%
    <sub>percent</sub>

10. 2.92 = _____%
    <sub>percent</sub>

11. .57 = _____%
    <sub>percent</sub>

12. 1.13 = _____%
    <sub>percent</sub>

# Add Zeros When Necessary

To change a decimal to a percent, move the decimal point two places to the right and add a percent symbol. You may need to add zeros to the **right** of the decimal point.

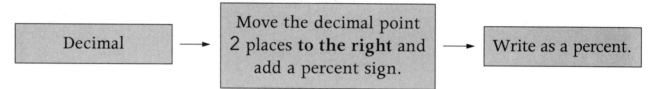

| Decimal | Move the decimal point 2 places **to the right** and add a percent sign. | Write as a percent. |

Example 1:    2        2.00%        200%

Example 2:    .9        .90%        90%

Example 3:    3.8        3.80%        380%

---

Write each decimal as a percent. Add zeros if necessary.

1.   .3 = _____ %
   <small>percent</small>

2.   .5 = _____ %
   <small>percent</small>

3.   3.4 = _____ %
   <small>percent</small>

4.   9.1 = _____ %
   <small>percent</small>

5.   .7 = _____ %
   <small>percent</small>

6.   8 = _____ %
   <small>percent</small>

7.   .8 = _____ %
   <small>percent</small>

8.   6 = _____ %
   <small>percent</small>

9.   .4 = _____ %
   <small>percent</small>

10.   5.9 = _____ %
   <small>percent</small>

11.   .1 = _____ %
   <small>percent</small>

12.   3.2 = _____ %
   <small>percent</small>

# Percents and Decimals Review

Write each percent as a decimal.

1. 157% = _____

2. 228% = _____

3. 911% = _____

4. 813% = _____

5. 456% = _____

Write each decimal as a percent.

6. .3 = _____ %

7. .5 = _____ %

8. 2.6 = _____ %

9. 5.4 = _____ %

10. 8 = _____ %

# Put It All Together

Step 1: Name the fractional part that is shaded.
Step 2: Rename as a decimal in hundredths.
Step 3: Write the percent.

**1.**

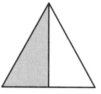

a) Fraction $\frac{1}{2}$

b) Decimal .50

c) Percent 50%

**2.**

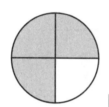

a) Fraction ⬜/⬜

b) Decimal _____

c) Percent _____%

**3.**

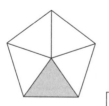

a) Fraction ⬜/⬜

b) Decimal _____

c) Percent _____%

**4.**

a) Fraction ⬜/⬜

b) Decimal _____

c) Percent _____%

**5.**

a) Fraction ⬜/⬜

b) Decimal _____

c) Percent _____%

**6.**

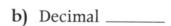

a) Fraction ⬜/⬜

b) Decimal _____

c) Percent _____%

# Equivalents

Start with the given amount. Use that amount to find equivalent fractions, decimals, or percents.

| | Fraction (simplified) | Fraction (hundredths) | Decimal | Percent |
|---|---|---|---|---|
| 1. | $\frac{1}{2}$ | $\frac{50}{100}$ | .**5 0** | **50** % |
| 2. | $\frac{\square}{\square}$ | $\frac{\square}{100}$ | .25 ← start here | ____ % |
| 3. | $\frac{\square}{\square}$ | $\frac{75}{100}$ ← start here | .____ | ____ % |
| 4. | $\frac{\square}{\square}$ | $\frac{\square}{100}$ | .____ | 10% |
| 5. | $\frac{7}{10}$ | $\frac{\square}{100}$ | .____ | ____ % |
| 6. | $\frac{\square}{\square}$ | $\frac{60}{100}$ | .____ | ____ % |
| 7. | $\frac{\square}{\square}$ | $\frac{\square}{100}$ | .40 | ____ % |
| 8. | $\frac{3}{10}$ | $\frac{\square}{100}$ | .____ | ____ % |
| 9. | $\frac{\square}{\square}$ | $\frac{\square}{100}$ | .02 | ____ % |
| 10. | $\frac{\square}{\square}$ | $\frac{\square}{100}$ | .____ | 20% |

# Comparing Percents, Fractions, and Decimals

Write < (less than), > (greater than), or = (equal to) in each circle to make each number statement true.

---

1. .6 $\overbrace{\phantom{.6}}$ ( = ) 60%
   Think:
   .6 = .60

2. 63% ( ) 1.00

3. $\frac{6}{100}$ ( ) .05

4. 50% ( ) $\frac{3}{5}$

5. $\frac{1}{4}$ ( ) .15

6. $\frac{1}{4}$ ( ) .30

7. 5% ( ) .5

8. .8 ( ) 75%

9. $\frac{1}{10}$ ( ) 10%

10. 30% ( ) .03

11. 5% ( ) $\frac{1}{5}$

12. $\frac{13}{20}$ ( ) 65%

# Using Proportions

To change a fraction to a percent, you must find how many hundredths the fraction represents. To do this you can use proportions. One of the ratios (fractions) in the proportion must have a denominator of 100.

> Remember: **Proportions** are two equivalent fractions.

EXAMPLE 1: Change $\frac{1}{5}$ to a percent.

Step 1: Set up a proportion.

$$\frac{1}{5} = \frac{n}{100}$$

*stands for unknown percent*

*percent is part of 100*

Step 2: Write the cross products.

$$\frac{1}{5} \diagup\!\!\!\!\diagdown \frac{n}{100}$$

$$1 \times 100 = n \times 5$$

Step 3: Multiply the two numbers in the cross product.

$$100 = n \times 5$$

Step 4: Divide by the third number to find what $n$ is.

$$100 \div 5 = n$$
$$20 = n$$

A. $\frac{1}{5} = \frac{n}{100} = \frac{20}{100}$ so $\frac{1}{5} = \underline{\ \ 20\ \ }$ %
<br>$\phantom{A. \frac{1}{5} = \frac{n}{100} = \frac{20}{100}} $ fill in

---

EXAMPLE 2: Change $\frac{2}{3}$ to a percent.

Step 1: Set up a proportion.

$$\frac{2}{3} = \frac{n}{100}$$

Step 2: Cross multiply.

$$2 \times 100 = n \times 3$$

Step 3: Multiply the two numbers.

$$\underline{\qquad}_{\text{fill in}} = n \times 3$$

Step 4: Divide by the third number.

$$\underline{\qquad}_{\text{fill in}} \div 3 = n$$

$$\underline{\qquad}_{\text{fill in}} = n$$

B. $\frac{2}{3} = \frac{n}{100} = \frac{66\frac{2}{3}}{100}$ so $\frac{2}{3} = \underline{\qquad}$ %
<br>$\phantom{B. \frac{2}{3} = \frac{n}{100}}$ fill in

# Use Cross Products

Use proportions to change the fractions to percents.

**1.** Change $\frac{1}{3}$ to a percent.

$$\frac{1}{3} \diagup\kern-1em= \frac{n}{100}$$

$$1 \times 100 = n \times 3$$

$$100 = n \times 3$$

$$100 \div 3 = n$$

$$33\frac{1}{3} = n$$

$$\frac{1}{3} = \frac{33\frac{1}{3}}{100} \quad \text{so} \quad \frac{1}{3} = \underline{\hspace{1.5cm}}\% $$
$$\text{\small fill in}$$

**2.** Change $\frac{1}{6}$ to a percent.

**3.** Change $\frac{7}{8}$ to a percent.

**4.** Change $\frac{5}{8}$ to a percent.

$$\frac{5}{8} \diagup\kern-1em= \frac{n}{100}$$

$$5 \times 100 = n \times 8$$

$$\underline{\hspace{1.5cm}} = n \times 8$$

$$\underline{\hspace{0.8cm}} \div \underline{\hspace{0.8cm}} = n$$

$$\underline{\hspace{0.8cm}}\frac{1}{2} = n$$

$$\frac{5}{8} = \frac{\phantom{xx}}{100} \quad \text{so} \quad \frac{5}{8} = \underline{\hspace{1.5cm}}\% $$
$$\text{\small fill in}$$

**5.** Change $\frac{1}{9}$ to a percent.

**6.** Change $\frac{5}{6}$ to a percent.

# Find the Percent

Use cross products to find the percent that is shaded.

**1.**

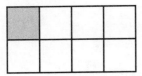

Shaded part $\longrightarrow$ $\dfrac{1}{8}$ $\diagdown$ $\dfrac{n}{100}$
Total parts $\longrightarrow$

$$1 \times 100 = n \times 8$$

$$100 = n \times 8$$

$$100 \div 8 = n$$

$$\underline{\hspace{2cm}} = n$$

$$\underline{\hspace{2cm}}\% = \dfrac{1}{8}$$

**2.**

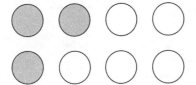

Shaded parts $\longrightarrow$ $\dfrac{3}{8}$ $\diagdown$ $\dfrac{n}{100}$
Total parts $\longrightarrow$

**3.**

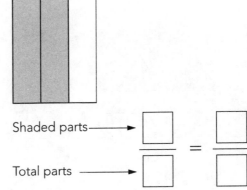

Shaded parts $\longrightarrow$ $\dfrac{\boxed{\phantom{0}}}{\boxed{\phantom{0}}} = \dfrac{\boxed{\phantom{0}}}{\boxed{\phantom{0}}}$
Total parts $\longrightarrow$

**4.**

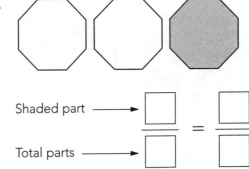

Shaded part $\longrightarrow$ $\dfrac{\boxed{\phantom{0}}}{\boxed{\phantom{0}}} = \dfrac{\boxed{\phantom{0}}}{\boxed{\phantom{0}}}$
Total parts $\longrightarrow$

# Picture These Percents

For each problem, name the fractional part that is shaded or circled. Then name it as a percent.

**1.**

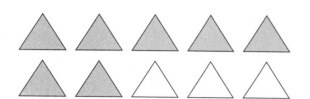

Parts shaded ⟶
Total parts ⟶ $\dfrac{7}{10} = \dfrac{\boxed{\phantom{0}}}{100} = $ _____ %

**2.**

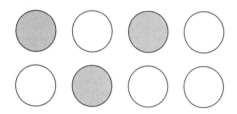

Parts shaded ⟶
Total parts ⟶ $\dfrac{\boxed{\phantom{0}}}{\boxed{\phantom{0}}} = \dfrac{\boxed{\phantom{0}}}{100} = $ _____ %

**3.**

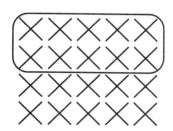

Parts circled ⟶
Total parts ⟶ $\dfrac{\boxed{\phantom{0}}}{\boxed{\phantom{0}}} = \dfrac{\boxed{\phantom{0}}}{100} = $ _____ %

**4.**

Parts shaded ⟶
Total parts ⟶ $\dfrac{\boxed{\phantom{0}}}{\boxed{\phantom{0}}} = \dfrac{\boxed{\phantom{0}}}{100} = $ _____ %

**5.**

Parts circled ⟶
Total parts ⟶ $\dfrac{\boxed{\phantom{0}}}{\boxed{\phantom{0}}} = \dfrac{\boxed{\phantom{0}}}{100} = $ _____ %

**6.**

Parts shaded ⟶
Total parts ⟶ $\dfrac{\boxed{\phantom{0}}}{\boxed{\phantom{0}}} = \dfrac{\boxed{\phantom{0}}}{100} = $ _____ %

# Decimals, Fractions, and Percents Review

Fill in the missing equivalents.

1. $\dfrac{7}{10} = \dfrac{\boxed{\phantom{0}}}{\boxed{\phantom{0}}} = .\underline{\ }\,\underline{\ } = \underline{\hspace{1cm}}\%$

6. Change $\dfrac{1}{8}$ to a percent.

Answer: \_\_\_\_\_%

2. $\dfrac{1}{2} = \dfrac{\boxed{\phantom{0}}}{\boxed{\phantom{0}}} = .\underline{\ }\,\underline{\ } = \underline{\hspace{1cm}}\%$

7. Change $\dfrac{4}{16}$ to a percent.

Answer: \_\_\_\_\_%

3. $\dfrac{5}{8} = \dfrac{\boxed{\phantom{0}}}{\boxed{\phantom{0}}} = .\underline{\ }\,\underline{\ } = \underline{\hspace{1cm}}\%$

8. Change $\dfrac{6}{8}$ to a percent.

Answer: \_\_\_\_\_%

4. Write $<$, $>$, or $=$.

.7 ◯ 75%

9. X  X  ⬭X  X⬭  X  X  X  X

Name the fractional part that is circled. Then name it as a percent.

Answer: \_\_\_\_\_  Answer: \_\_\_\_\_%

5. Write $<$, $>$, or $=$.

34% ◯ .3

10. ⬤ ⬤ ⬤ ◯ ◯

Name the fractional part that is shaded. Then name it as a percent.

Answer: \_\_\_\_\_  Answer: \_\_\_\_\_%

# Mixed Review

For each problem, write a fraction, decimal, and percent that represent each drawing.

| | Fraction | Decimal (hundredths) | Percent |
|---|---|---|---|

**1.** Shaded squares to total squares

$\dfrac{3}{5}$    _____    _____

**2.** Indicated units to total units

$\dfrac{\boxed{\phantom{0}}}{\boxed{\phantom{0}}}$    _____    _____

**3.** Shaded circle to total circles

$\dfrac{\boxed{\phantom{0}}}{\boxed{\phantom{0}}}$    _____    _____

**4.** Shaded part to total

$\dfrac{\boxed{\phantom{0}}}{\boxed{\phantom{0}}}$    _____    _____

**5.** Part shaded to total

$\dfrac{\boxed{\phantom{0}}}{\boxed{\phantom{0}}}$    _____    _____

**6.** Shaded boxes to total boxes

$\dfrac{\boxed{\phantom{0}}}{\boxed{\phantom{0}}}$    _____    _____

**7.** Part shaded to total

$\dfrac{\boxed{\phantom{0}}}{\boxed{\phantom{0}}}$    _____    _____

**8.** Part shaded to total

$\dfrac{\boxed{\phantom{0}}}{\boxed{\phantom{0}}}$    _____    _____

# Change Fractions to Percents

Use the proportion method (page 55) or your memory of common equivalents (page 34) to write the fractions as percents.

1. $\frac{3}{4} = \dfrac{\boxed{\phantom{00}}}{100}$

   ___75___ hundredths = _____%

2. $\frac{1}{3} = \dfrac{\boxed{\phantom{00}}}{100}$

   _____ hundredths = _____%

3. $\frac{4}{5} = \dfrac{\boxed{\phantom{00}}}{100}$

   _____ hundredths = _____%

4. $\frac{2}{25} = \dfrac{\boxed{\phantom{00}}}{100}$

   _____ hundredths = _____%

5. $\frac{3}{8} = \dfrac{\boxed{\phantom{00}}}{100}$

   _____ hundredths = _____%

6. $\frac{9}{10} = \dfrac{\boxed{\phantom{00}}}{100}$

   _____ hundredths = _____%

7. $\frac{5}{6} = \dfrac{\boxed{\phantom{00}}}{100}$

   _____ hundredths = _____%

8. $\frac{5}{8} = \dfrac{\boxed{\phantom{00}}}{100}$

   _____ hundredths = _____%

9. $\frac{2}{3} = \dfrac{\boxed{\phantom{00}}}{100}$

   _____ hundredths = _____%

10. $\frac{1}{6} = \dfrac{\boxed{\phantom{00}}}{100}$

    _____ hundredths = _____%

# Using Division

Sometimes you may decide to change a fraction to a percent by using division.

Step 1: Write the fraction as a division problem.

Step 2: Divide to the hundredths place.

Step 3: Change the decimal to a percent by moving the decimal point two places to the right.

| EXAMPLE | STEP 1 | STEP 2 | STEP 3 |
|---|---|---|---|
| Change $\frac{1}{5}$ to a percent. | Think division. | Divide to the hundredths place. | Change to a percent. |
| | $\frac{1}{5}$ | $\begin{array}{r} .20 \\ 5\overline{)1.00} \end{array}$ | $.20 = 20\%$ |

|  |  | Divide | Change to a Percent |
|---|---|---|---|
| 1. $\frac{3}{10}$ | $\frac{3}{10}$ | $10\overline{)3.00}$ | $. \underline{3}\ \underline{0} = \underline{\hphantom{00}}\%$ |
| 2. $\frac{9}{10}$ | | | $. \underline{\hphantom{0}}\ \underline{\hphantom{0}} = \underline{\hphantom{00}}\%$ |
| 3. $\frac{3}{4}$ | | | $. \underline{\hphantom{0}}\ \underline{\hphantom{0}} = \underline{\hphantom{00}}\%$ |
| 4. $\frac{3}{5}$ | | | $. \underline{\hphantom{0}}\ \underline{\hphantom{0}} = \underline{\hphantom{00}}\%$ |
| 5. $\frac{1}{2}$ | | | $. \underline{\hphantom{0}}\ \underline{\hphantom{0}} = \underline{\hphantom{00}}\%$ |

# Working with Remainders

Some decimal division problems will have remainders.

Step 1: Divide to the hundredths place.

Step 2: Write the remainder as a fraction.

Step 3: Change the decimal and fraction remainder to a percent.

| EXAMPLE | STEP 1 | STEP 2 | STEP 3 |
|---|---|---|---|
| Change $\frac{1}{8}$ to a percent. | Divide to the hundredths place. | Write the remainder as a fraction and simplify when necessary. | Change to a percent. |

$$8\overline{)1.00}\phantom{0} \begin{array}{r} .12 \\ \underline{8\phantom{.}} \\ 20 \\ \underline{16} \\ 4 \end{array}$$

$$8\overline{)1.00}\,.12\tfrac{4}{8} = .12\tfrac{1}{2}$$

$$.12\tfrac{1}{2} = 12\tfrac{1}{2}\%$$

---

|  |  | | **Divide** | **Change to a Percent** |
|---|---|---|---|---|
| 1. | $\frac{7}{8}$ | $\frac{7}{8}$ | $8\overline{)7.00}$ | $.\_\_\ \_\_\ \dfrac{\Box}{\Box} = \_\_\_\_\%$ |
| 2. | $\frac{3}{8}$ | | | $.\_\_\ \_\_\ \dfrac{\Box}{\Box} = \_\_\_\_\%$ |
| 3. | $\frac{5}{8}$ | | | $.\_\_\ \_\_\ \dfrac{\Box}{\Box} = \_\_\_\_\%$ |
| 4. | $\frac{1}{9}$ | | | $.\_\_\ \_\_\ \dfrac{\Box}{\Box} = \_\_\_\_\%$ |
| 5. | $\frac{2}{3}$ | | | $.\_\_\ \_\_\ \dfrac{\Box}{\Box} = \_\_\_\_\%$ |
| 6. | $\frac{5}{6}$ | | | $.\_\_\ \_\_\ \dfrac{\Box}{\Box} = \_\_\_\_\%$ |

# Mixed Numbers to Percents

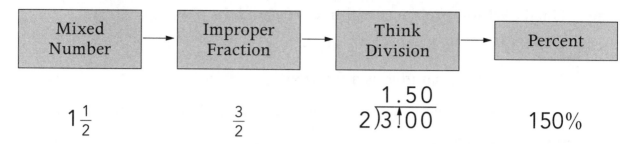

| Mixed Number | Improper Fraction | Think Division | Percent |
|:---:|:---:|:---:|:---:|
| $1\frac{1}{2}$ | $\frac{3}{2}$ | $2\overline{)3\phantom{.}00}^{\,1.50}$ | 150% |

Follow the steps to change each fraction to a percent.

| | Mixed Number | Improper Fraction | Think Division | Write Percent |
|:---:|:---:|:---:|:---:|:---:|
| 1. | $3\frac{3}{4}$ | $\dfrac{\square}{\square}$ | $\overline{)\phantom{xxxx}}$ | _ _ _ % |
| 2. | $2\frac{1}{3}$ | $\dfrac{\square}{\square}$ | | $\_\,\_\,\_\,\dfrac{\square}{\square}$ % |
| 3. | $4\frac{1}{2}$ | $\dfrac{\square}{\square}$ | | _ _ _ % |
| 4. | $3\frac{5}{6}$ | $\dfrac{\square}{\square}$ | | $\_\,\_\,\_\,\dfrac{\square}{\square}$ % |
| 5. | $2\frac{7}{8}$ | $\dfrac{\square}{\square}$ | | $\_\,\_\,\_\,\dfrac{\square}{\square}$ % |
| 6. | $6\frac{1}{4}$ | $\dfrac{\square}{\square}$ | | _ _ _ % |

The Meaning of Percent

# Use the Symbols

Without changing the fractions to percents, can you tell which fractions are greater than 100%, less than 100%, or equal to 100%?

| Number Relations Symbols |
| :--- |
| < is less than |
| > is greater than |
| = is equal to |

1. $\frac{3}{2}$ ( > ) 100%

2. $\frac{2}{3}$ ( ) 100%

3. $\frac{15}{16}$ ( ) 100%

4. $\frac{8}{8}$ ( ) 100%

5. $\frac{42}{40}$ ( ) 100%

6. $\frac{7}{8}$ ( ) 100%

7. $\frac{10}{9}$ ( ) 100%

8. $\frac{99}{101}$ ( ) 100%

9. $\frac{7}{6}$ ( ) 100%

10. $\frac{18}{7}$ ( ) 100%

11. $\frac{42}{49}$ ( ) 100%

12. $\frac{200}{100}$ ( ) 100%

13. $\frac{5}{8}$ ( ) 100%

14. $\frac{20}{19}$ ( ) 100%

15. $\frac{6}{1}$ ( ) 100%

16. $\frac{21}{21}$ ( ) 100%

# More Fractions and Percents Review

Use the proportion method to write the fractions as percents.

1. $\dfrac{3}{25}$ = $\dfrac{\Box}{100}$

   _____ hundredths = _____ %

2. $\dfrac{1}{5}$ = $\dfrac{\Box}{100}$

   _____ hundredths = _____ %

Change each mixed number to a percent.

3. $4\dfrac{1}{3}$

4. $2\dfrac{5}{8}$

Change each fraction to a percent using the division method.

5. $\dfrac{1}{5}$

6. $\dfrac{3}{8}$

7. $\dfrac{3}{5}$

8. $\dfrac{8}{10}$

# Understanding Percents

In Jorie's English class, 8 out of 12 students are female.

1. Write a simplified fraction:  $\frac{8}{12} = \frac{2}{3}$

2. Write as a decimal:  $\frac{2}{3} = .66\frac{2}{3}$

3. Write as a percent:  $66\frac{2}{3}\%$

$$\underset{\text{fraction}}{\frac{2}{3}} \qquad \underset{\text{decimal}}{.66\frac{2}{3}} \qquad \underset{\text{percent}}{66\frac{2}{3}\%}$$

---

Write each relationship as a simplified fraction, decimal, and percent.

1. Carrie missed 2 out of 20 problems on a test.

$$\frac{\Box}{\Box} = \frac{\Box}{\Box} \qquad .\underline{\phantom{x}}\,\underline{\phantom{x}} \quad \underline{\phantom{xx}}\%$$
$$\underset{\text{fraction}}{} \qquad \underset{\text{decimal}}{} \quad \underset{\text{percent}}{}$$

4. 3 out 4 students ride the bus to school.

$$\frac{\Box}{\Box} \qquad .\underline{\phantom{x}}\,\underline{\phantom{x}} \quad \underline{\phantom{xx}}\%$$

2. Janet spent 6 out of 24 hours sleeping.

$$\frac{\Box}{\Box} = \frac{\Box}{\Box} \qquad .\underline{\phantom{x}}\,\underline{\phantom{x}} \quad \underline{\phantom{xx}}\%$$

5. 8 out of 10 homes have a DVD player.

$$\frac{\Box}{\Box} = \frac{\Box}{\Box} \qquad .\underline{\phantom{x}}\,\underline{\phantom{x}} \quad \underline{\phantom{xx}}\%$$

3. Susie made 9 out of 10 free throws.

$$\frac{\Box}{\Box} \qquad .\underline{\phantom{x}}\,\underline{\phantom{x}} \quad \underline{\phantom{xx}}\%$$

6. Kevin spent $10 out of $30.

$$\frac{\Box}{\Box} = \frac{\Box}{\Box} \qquad .\underline{\phantom{x}}\,\underline{\phantom{x}} \quad \underline{\phantom{xx}}\%$$

# Explain the Meaning

Explain what these percents mean in your own words.

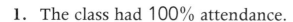

1. The class had 100% attendance.

   <u>All students were in the class.</u>

   _____

2.

   _____

   _____

3. Allen gave the waitress a 15% tip.

   _____

   _____

4.  A discount is how much something is reduced in price.

   _____

   _____

5. Clothing label

   | 35% Wool |
   | 65% Cotton |

   _____

   _____

6. 90% of the students passed the test.

   _____

   _____

7. Food prices increased 10% in one year.

   _____

   _____

8. A commission is an amount of money paid for selling goods.

   | Commission 20% |

   _____

# Percents of a Circle

All the percents in a circle must add up to 100%. Fill in the missing percents in the circles.

**1.** Halves

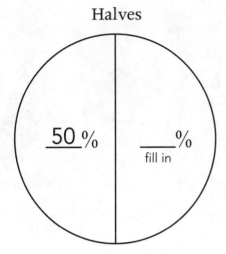

**2.** Thirds

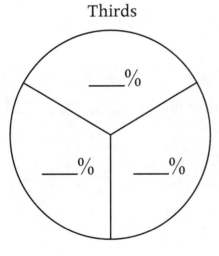

**3.** Fourths

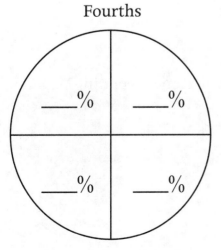

**4.** Fifths

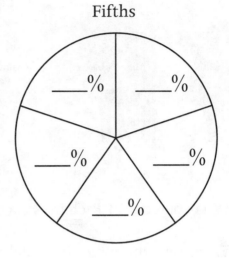

**5.** Eighths

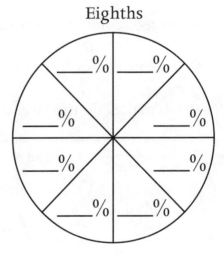

**6.** Tenths

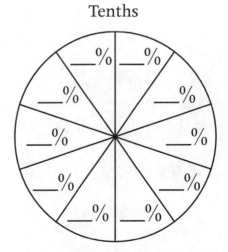

# Circle Graphs

Circle graphs show relationships of parts of a whole (100%). They make it easy to compare the sizes of different parts.

## Richard's Earnings

  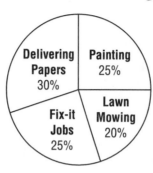  

1.  What percent of Richard's earnings comes from mowing lawns? _____%

2.  What percent comes from delivering papers? _____%

3.  What percent comes from painting? _____%

4.  What percent comes from fix-it jobs? _____%

5.  What job makes up the largest percent of his earnings? _____

## Mrs. Gomez's Budget

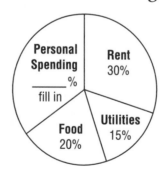

6.  What percent of Mrs. Gomez's budget is for personal spending? _____%

7.  $\frac{1}{5}$ of the budget is for _____. (Think: $\frac{1}{5}$ = ?%)

8.  $\frac{3}{10}$ of the budget is for _____.

9.  $\frac{3}{20}$ of the budget is for _____.

10. The smallest percent of her spending is for _____.

# Practice Your Skills

1. Draw a circle around 60% of the Xs.

2. In the space at the right,
   draw 5 circles.
   Shade in 40% of them.

3. What percent of the
   triangles is shaded? _____

4. The statement: "1 out of 3" is represented by what percent? _____

5. What percent is shaded? _____

6. What percent is not shaded? _____

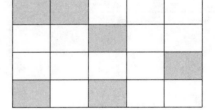

7. What percent is shaded? _____

8. What percent is not shaded? _____

9. What percent is circled? _____

10. What percent is not circled? _____

# Percent Review

**1.** What percent of the circles is shaded? _____ %

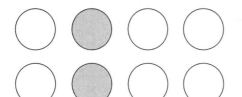

**2.** What percent of the rectangle is shaded? _____ %

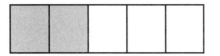

**3.** What percent of the line has been marked off? _____ %

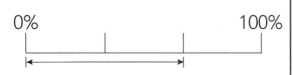

**4.** Shade 80% of the squares.

**5.** Shade 25% of the 12 squares.

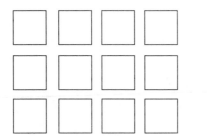

Fill in the equivalent values.

| Fraction (simplified) | Decimal (hundredths) | Percent (out of 100) |
|---|---|---|
| **6.** $\frac{1}{2}$ | . _ _ | _____ % |
| **7.** $\frac{\square}{\square}$ | . _ _ | 25% |
| **8.** $\frac{\square}{\square}$ | .30 | _____ % |
| **9.** $\frac{3}{4}$ | . _ _ | _____ % |
| **10.** $\frac{\square}{\square}$ | . _ _ | 20% |
| **11.** $\frac{3}{8}$ | . _ _ $\frac{\square}{\square}$ | _____ % |
| **12.** $\frac{\square}{\square}$ | .05 | _____ % |
| **13.** $\frac{\square}{\square}$ | . _ _ | 1% |
| **14.** $\frac{1}{8}$ | . _ _ $\frac{\square}{\square}$ | _____ % |
| **15.** $\frac{1}{3}$ | . _ _ $\frac{\square}{\square}$ | _____ % |

# Real-Life Percents

Solve each problem.

1. If 100% of the 27 students were in class, how many students were there?

   Answer: _____

2. A $100 jacket is on sale for $\frac{1}{2}$ off. What is the percent off?

   Answer: _____%

3. If 50% of the 30 students passed the test, what fraction passed the test?

   Answer: $\frac{\boxed{\phantom{0}}}{\boxed{\phantom{0}}}$

4. If $\frac{2}{3}$ of the cake is gone, what percent is gone?

   Answer: _____%

5. 75% of the seats are taken. What fraction of the seats are taken?

   Answer: $\frac{\boxed{\phantom{0}}}{\boxed{\phantom{0}}}$

6. Only $\frac{2}{5}$ of the flights are on time. What percent of flights are on time?

   Answer: _____%

7. There are $2\frac{1}{3}$ pizzas on the table. What percent of pizzas are on the table?

   Answer: _____%

8. 50% of the 10 employees called in sick. How many people called in sick?

   Answer: _____

# Real-Life Percents Review

Explain the meaning.

**1.** The pudding is 2% sugar.

_____

_____

_____

**2.** Jimmy got a 10% bonus.

_____

_____

_____

**3.** 50% of the milk was gone.

_____

_____

_____

**4.** Jenny scored 100%.

_____

_____

_____

Solve each problem.

**5.** 25% of the problems were wrong. What fraction of the problems were wrong?

Answer: $\dfrac{\Box}{\Box}$

**6.** $\frac{1}{5}$ of the budget is for food. What percent is for food?

Answer: _____ %

**7.** 60% of the students ate a bag lunch. What fraction ate a bag lunch?

Answer: $\dfrac{\Box}{\Box}$

**8.** $\frac{2}{3}$ of the money was saved. What percent was saved?

Answer: _____ %

# The Meaning of Percents Review

Solve each problem.

1. 25% means:

   a) 4 out of _____

   b) 10 out of _____

2. Write the fraction or the percent.

   a) $20\% = \dfrac{\Box}{\Box}$

   b) $\dfrac{1}{3} = $ _____%

3. Write as a fraction or mixed number.

   a) $46\% = $ _____

   b) $105\% = $ _____

   c) $350\% = $ _____

   d) $142\% = $ _____

4. Change each decimal to a percent.

   a) $.1 = $ _____%     b) $.9 = $ _____%     c) $.3 = $ _____%

5. Use division to change each fraction to a percent.

   a) $\dfrac{2}{3} = $ _____%

   b) $\dfrac{1}{2} = $ _____%

   c) $\dfrac{1}{4} = $ _____%

   d) $\dfrac{1}{3} = $ _____%

1. Change .65 to a percent.

   Answer: _____

2. 18% means _____ out of 100.

   Answer: _____

3. Write $\frac{1}{5}$ as a percent.

   Answer: _____

4. Juanita spends $2 out of every $5 that she earns on food. What percent of her income does she spend on food?

   Answer: _____

5. Change 24% to a fraction and simplify.

   Answer: _____

6. Write 1.39 as a percent.

   Answer: _____

7. Change $2\frac{3}{5}$ to a percent.

   Answer: _____

8. 85 out of 100 is the same as _____%.

   Answer: _____

9. Change $\frac{5}{8}$ to a percent.

   Answer: _____

10. The whole number 3 is the same as _____%.

   Answer: _____

11. Change 450% to a mixed number and simplify.

Answer: _____

12. Write $\frac{3}{20}$ as a percent.

Answer: _____

13. Serena got 4 problems right out of every 5 on her math test. What percent of the problems did she get right?

Answer: _____

14. Write the whole number 6 as a percent.

Answer: _____

15. Change .025 to a percent.

Answer: _____

16. Write 7% as a decimal.

Answer: _____

17. 19 out of every 20 employees in Dave's shop drive to work. What percent of the employees drive to work?

Answer: _____

18. Write $\frac{7}{10}$ as a percent.

Answer: _____

19. Change .29 to a percent.

Answer: _____

20. Riley got 3 hits out of every 8 times he was at bat. What percent of the time did he get a hit?

Answer: _____

# Evaluation Chart

On the following chart, circle the number of any problem you missed. The column after the problem number tells you the pages where those problems are taught. You should review the sections for any problem you missed.

| Skill Area | Posttest Problem Number | Skill Section | Review Page |
|---|---|---|---|
| Meaning of Percent | 2, 8, 10 | 7–17 | 18 |
| Fractions and Percent | 3, 5, 9, 12, 18 | 19–34<br>61–65 | 35<br>66 |
| Percents Greater Than 100 | 7, 11, 14 | 36–40 | 41 |
| Percents and Decimals | 15, 16, 19 | 42–50 | 51 |
| Decimals, Fractions, and Percents | 1, 6 | 52–58 | 59 |
| Percent Problem Solving | 4, 13, 17, 20 | 67–73 | 74 |

**attendance**   the number of people at an event

  Attendance at the football game was 450.

**budget**   a plan for spending money

  I wrote a budget so I could save money.

**commission**   money paid to a sales person for his or her services, or money paid to a sales person based on the amount of items he or she sells

  John earns a 20% commission on everything he sells.

**denominator**   the bottom part of a fraction

  $\frac{5}{8} \leftarrow$

**discount**   the reduced cost of an item

  I bought my suit at a discount store to save money.

**earnings**   salary, wages, or income

  My earnings for this year are $23,000.00

**equivalent**   two numbers that have the same value

  $\frac{1}{3} = \frac{2}{6}$

**improper fraction**   a fraction where the numerator is greater than the denominator

  The improper fraction $\frac{7}{5}$ can be rewritten as $1\frac{2}{7}$.

**mixed number**   the combination of a whole number and a fraction

  $2\frac{1}{2}$ is a mixed number

**number relation symbol**   symbols that explain the relationship between two numbers

  For example:

  | | |
  |---|---|
  | less than | $<$ |
  | greater than | $>$ |
  | is equal to | $=$ |
  | not equal to | $\neq$ |

  15 is greater than 9
    **OR**
  $15 > 9$

**percent**   a way of expressing a number as the part of a whole; the word *percent* means *out of 100*

  José answered 40 questions correct out of 50. What percent did he answer correctly?

  $\frac{40}{50} = \frac{n}{100}$

  $n = 80\%$

**ratio**   a comparison of two numbers

  If John strikes out 2 of every 3 batters, the ratio of strikes to hits is 2:3.

**remainder**   the number that is left over when a division problem doesn't divide evenly

$$\overset{\displaystyle\downarrow}{\overset{4\,\text{R}1}{4\overline{)17}}}$$

**rename**   to change a mixed or whole number into a fraction

$$5 = \frac{25}{5} \qquad 1 = \frac{7}{7}$$

**simplify (reduce)**   to make the number in a fraction smaller without changing the value of the fraction

$$\frac{2}{4} = \frac{1}{2} \qquad \frac{4}{6} = \frac{2}{3}$$

**tip**   money left for a waiter or waitress

My lunch cost $6.25 and I left $1.00 for a tip.